W9-CWW-268

Larry Rubin

ALL MY MIRRORS LIE

DAVID R. GODINE

BOSTON

David R. Godine, Publisher
Boston, Massachusetts

LCC 74-25956
ISBN 0-87923-120-3
Printed in the United States of America

Acknowledgments: 'Postmortem' first appeared in *Chicago Review*. 'The Bachelor: First Routine Check-up' first appeared in *Esquire*. 'The Brother-in-Law, Reconciled' first appeared in *North American Review*. 'Curtains of the Sea' first appeared in *Poetry*. 'Toward Night' first appeared in *Prairie Schooner*. 'The Mute, Swimming' and 'The Voyage' first appeared in the *Sewanee Review* 78 (1970), and 'Total Recall' and 'The Bachelor, at Sea' first appeared in the *Sewanee Review* 80 (1972); copyright 1970, 1972 by the University of the South. Other poems in this book appeared in: *American Review*, *Antaeus*, *Carleton Miscellany*, *Das Pult*, *Denver Quarterly*, *Encounter*, *Harper's Magazine*, *Kansas Quarterly*, *Kenyon Review*, *The Nation*, *New American Review*, *New York Quarterly*, *Quarterly Review of Literature*, *Red Clay Reader*, *Southern Review*, *Southwest Review*, *Transatlantic Review*, *University of Windsor Review*, *Vanderbilt Poetry Review*, *Virginia Quarterly Review*, *Yale Review*.

A Godine Poetry Chapbook
Second Series

All My Mirrors Lie

Part One: The Farther Side Of Music

Letters from Abroad

Suburban symbols:
A mailbox on a graveyard wall
Brooding on the snow, bone-white
In street-light,
Waiting for some ghost
Who forgot to write;
Wakened in guilt
From her school of dreams
She hurries down the phantom walk
Slipping on black ice,
But floats the final distance
Detaching from her shroud
A square of white
And slips it through the slot of ice.

I wake in cold electric light
Draining the dark of a waning dream;
The snow floats nameless toward the farthest wall.
I hurry for the morning mail.

At the Birth of the Composer

On the farther side of music
Where the notes are still untoned
The atoms once were flesh or forest
And the slumber of the horns

Veiled my mother's face in shadow;
She felt the strings at the vibrant core,
Coronets for hidden suns—
Paths of reeds led past the stars

Where she gathered all her music,
Tympanies of perforated
Thunder, silence in her ears
At dawn. And when her pulse of weighted

Movements led her to the wood,
I was born this side of music,
Deafened in the halls of blood.

Radio Engineering
(*A Note on the Immortality of Electrical Impulses*)

Emblem of invisibles, the air
Relays a music mediated far
By harps and cellos plucked from stations zoned
For chamber groups and lunar marathons.

Infinity's plus-and-minus cells, the brain
Pulses the keys, telepathy's half-tones;
Beyond Jupiter the signals seem to fade,
But antennas lengthen when the eye corrodes.

The busy air's high season: death—
Another fugue, played on subtracted breath.

A Note on Medical Progress (Cardiac Division)

Now they're making artificial hearts
And when I heard the news
At first I thought, 'Wait until *she* hears,'
Before I remembered. Now

It's too late for electronic parts, but something's pumping
Blood into her crumbled veins
Somewhere. Once the doctors spoke of clamping
The ventricle to lanes

Of nylon, but that was dashed before they dared.
No, this was something different:
As if a vision—not a dream—had veered
Behind my eyes, she bent

Her face toward mine, and candles lit that flesh
In pores of light; she used
Up all her batteries to smile, as rash
As the little girl who froze

After striking all her matches in the snow
To see her grandmother's face.
Before the circuits broke, I felt the thaw
Her heart had bought; I knew the price.

A View from Above the Town

The light is enough. I will earn it
With my life, and leave the curve of time.
It comes now, misted in November,
Pale silk above the hills, saffron
Through the cellophane of cloud. Refractions
Fool me into seeing cars below,
Houses, streets and trees, the flesh of men.
My body knows itself a lump in light
And strains for dissolution, separating
Petals from an empty stem, weightless
Nectar scattered to the stars. The day
I sleep in light, these drops will blend.
                                                            The cloud
Darkens—I see no shelter on this hill.
The light will be enough, when I descend.

Outward Bound

It's the memories that project themselves
When nerves and cells have failed
Not the cheating touch
The flash of flesh
Your skin on skis
Misting the sea
Not the cavalcade of color
The rainbow spots around the disk
That flare their cones upon the stage
Nor the cradled warmth that body arcs can make
When reach and grasp connect
Protrusions lock in place
But what you can remember
After the final wave has passed
When the wheel of colored cellophane
Has spun beyond your retina
And flesh is something only bones define
Then you will slide on seas that have no temperature
Flashing through the spindrift in your brain
Spiraling through the arcs of time
Past forgotten barriers
Towards music
                    ether
                              waves of light

Part Two: Slitting the Seal of Infinity

The Manual

I found it in the bottom drawer
Under her wedding linen
And reading it was like eating the wild apples
That grew in my grandfather's orchard
Till I was sick with ferment and love
And ran for relief, racing the rain in my bowels
But now my canals were thick with the freight of their
 fourteen years
And the dreams came thick and heavy
At the point where dew descends
At the moment of belief in those printed words
When the diagrams exploded in my dreams

And I was putting the book back in the drawer
Under her wedding linen
When she came in and saw me
And asked if I understood
Smoothing the folds in something she'd bought as a bride
I saw the bewilderment in my mother's eyes
And quietly closed the drawer, and lied

Total Recall

A bag of ragged nerves and wormy fruit,
My brain was overloaded—overstocked
With every raw-boned image of my mother
Staring into the mirror of her vanity—
My father sleeping in a darkened room
During the drowsy lunchtime break,
My nectarines descending in the bowl
As I watched the worm uncoil its naked length,
Seeing Sister hug her breasts and float
Right out the door on someone's flying worm—

I registered this freight, and stored it live,
Thought to market memories, marked it
'Perishable.' But it fermented in the cars,
Swelled up and cracked the crates, and split my brain.
The nectarines are spoiled. I count the worms.

Geometry Test
(Tenth Grade)

Thirty minutes, we had, to prove the theorem.
For twenty I sat staring at circles,
My inner angles frozen
When nothing came out equal.
The bisectors I drew were tilted wrong
While fear of the circular face of time
Stiffened my blood like clock-hands
Tracing arcs I never knew existed.
Suddenly that curve stretched perpendicular—
Longer than my longest transverse line—
Reaching beyond the limits of the page;
And the tallest segments of the intersected cone
Slit the seal of infinity.

My mind was washed like windshields after rain
And circles glided smoothly into place,
The arcs connecting in their shrunken frames.
I left that room, all theorems proved.

Greying

'When you get grey, I bet you'll dye your hair,'
My father said, letting his short locks
Whiten as they would, and proud of it.
The tone was knowledge, half unknown, a taunt
To the unnatural elements that haunt
A father when his son is not a father
Too. 'The sun may bleach it just a shade,'
I said. 'You know I ramble on the beach
A lot—but never dye. Why should I?'
He died, and I was suddenly his age. On the beach
I saw how dark the lovers were
Where everything lay curled, and felt the ache
Of ice sprouting from my scalp. I wanted
Arms, an end to ice, and dipped my hair
In the blackest ink that love provides,
Combing the beach until my father cried.

The Revenge

I drive him deeper into Hell each time,
Seeking the shape that ruptured into seed—

Father, you could not stand the strain of love
And hid your loins from my lean hands.
How could I be what I never saw, or touched?
Lost in that cylinder of lust, I dreamed
Of rough-house with our fountain man,
Rising horseplay in the boarder's bath;
All transients, drifters, vagrant loves
Loiter in my brain—I use your coins
To purchase what I never knew was there.

The Revenge (II)

The sound of sleet at three a.m.—
Some cold assassin placing his ladder softly
Against the side of the house, awaking the white
Side of my brain, which slips from sleep and pushes
The pillow to the cooler half. I was dreaming
Of my father's bones, touching his cold mouth
With fingers like a child's soda straw;
Then the ice cream fell in noisy flakes
And his bones were climbing ladders to my room—
Dripping sleet, he sought my bed. I sucked
The leavings in the empty glass, and slept.

Part Three: Lured into the Crucible

The Bachelor, at Sea

Lying there, dead between the worlds,
As we rocked
He asked me about love;
It was all in sleep and I could answer
As I pleased,
Knowing his world could never touch mine.
Dark goes to light, he said, and winked,
And I felt the water rush beneath the ship in sleep,
The frenzied waves fusing in their own likeness,
A mirrored chase deep into horizon's halls.
I wanted to explain, as fathers do to sons,
But he was waiting for my body
To redesign that old design,
Renew his face, that ran like water in my dream:
My prince, my father, pattern of my drowned desire.

The Looting

This parish has been plundered
The poets have been here
Ransacking, ruining, denuding
Everything worth taking is gone
Sequestered pools polluted
The tallest oaks defrocked
The very skies defiled
Stars destroyed
Vandals filching
Locusts flashing
(That girl on the urn
Has thighs made of stone)
Flesh they turn to foam
And hurl the lovers from a cliff they've made
I've seen them disembowel the sun

Nothing is safe
I woke this morning thinking of someone I swore I'd
never mention
Just out of public decency
He was already in a poem

The Bachelor, as Professor

My sons are always young—
The liquid flowers of their eyes may change
But the light remains.
Their names are always on the chart
Spelled differently year by year
(In rollbooks of my mind
I can correct what seems irregular).
I cannot age.
Waves of time dissolve that flare of faces
Every spring, yet the waters bloom again
With eyes: I swim toward them, an athlete at last.
Though I reach for them invisibly, in voice,
Any bell is strong enough to break that bond—
But when they're safe at home and sipping soup
And telling body parents how they mean to thrive,
Their eyes are fixed upon unborn designs:
Their words are mine.

Toward Night

Only elemental things are left
Saturday afternoons. To phone a friend
Will bring metallic endless rings, until
My hand grows weary with the weight.
O they have gone, where blood and sperm have curved
Their lives, to hills where bridegrooms play, to arcs
That widen into wombs, where children dance.
The streets I walk are emptied of the week.
Only elemental sunlight stays
And something as a child I called the sky—
An endlessness of space I thought was blue.
The elemental trees release their leaves
In primary tones I learned when I was eight.
The sea is grieving for its loss, the waves
Remembering a hand I think was mine.
Woven into all these things, the wind
Makes love to leaves, and spins away the foam
From old forgotten waves, then whistles toward
The sky. Upon a marble wall the sun
Falls red.
I release the phone and wait
For dark. The element of blood begins.

Nightmare of a Bachelor

Awakened at night by sounds of rattled leaves
Trembling on the tree like tambourines—
Every place a pulse was ever heard
Humming like electrodes in the heart,
I lie stiff, afraid to look at darkness,
Afraid to turn toward darkness, the monster shapes
Of coats on doors, of swollen chairs, mirrors
That may suddenly reflect their dead;
All engines stopped, for silent ship,
I wait for ghosts to glide like submarines
Past my point of danger; no other breath
Upon the bed, no other arms, I ride
The draining seas of night, awaiting the alarm.

To a Friend Who Has Just Returned

Where were you, the last five years,
Burrowing into life, with rumors of ships
And voyages, the fog-deflected horns on seas
I could only wade in, on deserted beaches—
Where were you, in cities arching past
Horizons, through unfamiliar hemispheres,
Bazaars and spices, the silence of fjords—
The naked parapets a passport buys—
While I, riveted to schedules, faced
The faces I could not hope would recognize
My love, that lapsed into forgetfulness
With each cold bell, and all I owned were books.
What was it you sought, and why do you sit now
Shivering on the parapet, awaiting
My cold touch, lured into
The crucible, these consuming poems?

The Bachelor, Waking

In bed it seems enormous with its need—
Not even fugues on the clock-radio
Relieve the flood, nor the full tide of sunlight
That drowns me in waves of thrust and burst;
Nor last night's memory of sloping stars,
The suns that wait beyond the falls of time,
Can fill the gaps that flash from groin to brain.
My body twists into the coverlets
That bulge their answers to the mirror's dream—
But then I stand, before the final crest
Has broken into foam; and blood withdraws
Beyond the fictions of the empty bed.

February Thaw

The day the snow is gone
The sun floating higher than it ever dared
Up a slope of blue
And yet before the birds
Or leaves
Your hands still huddled in your coat
You must take the branches as design
Tangled signatures against the sky
Illegible
Yet dancing even in their stillness
Naked patterns
Too thin to hide the lovers
Moving like tall music on the staff
Exposed, if you look too close
Betrayed by wordless branches
Shivering on the hill
Waiting for April
Too soon for leaves to cover love

Designs of empty branches
Signatures not your own
Signing the complaint

The Correspondent

I answer letters, having only words
For my embrace, and flutter on the fringe
Of fantasy, on wings the minds of men
Have fashioned out of sounds deeper than
The depth of stones or water, deeper than death.
I answer letters, that the flights in fall
Of birds departing may reflect with sweep
And speed the thoughts of my responding flesh,
My trembling blood. For me to touch the wind
Is mute desire, a music in the bone.
I answer letters; delivered past all loss,
I watch you read, exposed, already braced.

Part Four: The Dark Side of the Moon

Annual Checkup

And I tire so easily, Doctor. Just reading
A few term papers, or two paltry
Hours telling what I know about
Life and art, God and man, and how
Each is a mirror of the other, or even
A simple spasm of my celibate
Canals, when I have glimpsed the dark side
Of the moon and questioned the chastity I once
Cherished—it's enough to break my back,
Almost; oh yes, I've tried the iron shots
And also vitamins, but this anemia
Is so pernicious, nothing seems to help;
Some precious vial of the spirit (a vile
Cliché—forgive me) has been spilled somewhere,
And prayers do seem so pointless. I mean, God
Is dead, and all (I read that somewhere), and all
My mirrors lie—I'm not that grey. The moon
Is coarse and crusted, Luna says, and this
I find depressing. Sometimes my students call
Me 'Sir' as if they mean it—is that a sign?
I scribble a little, but who reads poetry
These days? A protein diet—a little sun?
I'll try, but I have dozed in whitest light,
Dreaming of pregnant virgins, the groins of gods.

Dinner at the Mongoloid's

She sat by me and eyed me craftily
Through eyes squeezed tight, two broken ovals,
While her mother went to wash the dishes, leaving
Us to get acquainted on the sofa.
My adult silence hung in empty air,
While she sat prettily, scrubbed and ribboned,
Smelling of soap, and waited for a question,
For visitors knew the rules. But I was dumb,
Feeling my words fall hollow through the ovals
Of her eyes, and she moved closer, turning
Her dented features toward my face, and said,
'I think you're very handsome.' I smiled, truncated,
Faceless, afraid of mirrors, chromosomes.

A Note on the Morality of Ignoring Deathbed Requests

Under duress of dying, the mind rejects
The words of life, and what has been enacted
On the boards of time. 'Burn my poems,'
The lady said, fingering the gown
She'd worn to seal her to the snow.
'Destroy my parchment tales,' a poet at court
Demanded, thinking of the shame of cocks
And hens, priests and nuns who breathed,
And loved. To enter eternity, words
That smack of witchcraft must descend to flames,
That poets may rise through purities to stars.

And what of us? Are we to roam in silence
Through the shifting scenes, on this revolving
Stage? Give us their words, and let us learn
The lines that we may speak. Burn the only
Script? They ask too much. Let them
Take their chances with the speechless gods.

Early Easter

If it sleets at Easter, all the symbols fail.
The sun's a corpse, and dogwood petals fall
In flutes of ice. That sprig of rebirth green
Grows back into a marble grave—what
Can rise beyond congested sieves of sky?

There is, of course, an equinoctial light
That lasts past six—for weather cannot change
The angle of our planetary bones.
Embryos are hidden in the snow—the children
Hunt for frozen shells. Latin bells

Are tolling through the muffled walls.
I've seen
The stones my daughter rolls, on this cold lawn.

The Bachelor: Routine Checkup

Red and yellow. My two specimens.
Sunshine in the cup, ruby in the tube.
My tubes flow with colors a flower would be proud
To flaunt toward any fascinated bee.
And they are warm, warm as my own unflagging
Heart, heroic in its stethoscopic
Tympanies, its thumped exactitudes.
The lab will give a good report on my rich
And mellow juices; health in these pipes—
The sparkle of purity, no trace of spirochetes.
Yet something lingers, undetermined still:
He used a rubber glove, but failed to test
Responses in protruding tubes, nor what
The nature of their warmest rising was.
Other fluids weren't mentioned. I didn't ask.

Part Five: Sharing with Sister

The Traveler
(For My Sister)

They say her blood collapsed, but I know better.
She clawed her cage until her fingers splayed
And felt the rage of death that daughters feel
When fathers find a mistress in the stars.
We spoke of poems on my visits to
Her cell, and she saw Father in my eyes,
Swallowed her tablets, and spoke the swollen lines,
Calmed again by sunlight, words that cushioned
The concussion in her skull. But when the lines
Collapsed, I was on continents unknown,
Linking words her veins could never spell.
Father I would not be, and blood and words
Slowed in their cold cycle, and were gone.

The Brother-in-Law

Haunt him, Mona! Haunt him, demon sister!
He who filled your bed for twenty years,
Inflating placentas, till you withered in
His bursting gifts, and burrowed into safer
Ground, he will betray those nights; he's found
A woman newer in the flesh, and has pushed
Your grave below his bed.
                                        They will wed,
But I who was your lover first, before
I knew what women hid—by the manhood
I had then, I conjure you to wall
Their nights, and lie between their straining parts.
Haunt him in his massive hour—
                                                child, I call.

The Brother-in-Law, Reconciled

Peace. Let there be peace
Between us. I will recall my curse. Your woman
Now is velvet, my sister's made of sticks.
I will come and taste your food, and smile
And kiss the mask of her who molds the bed.
Let us chat of time and wills, children
Making nice adjustments. I see their eyes
And they see mine. They shake the wedding box
And kiss. We know the size, the shape, of sticks.

The Druggist's Daughter

Her tablets were always deeper than her dreams
And Father was a whisper waiting there at the end,
The hero of the heroin ride, stabbed to death
By needles fragile as my sister's eyes.
She wove them deep into her bones, heirlooms
Treasured more than children's toys, or pearls
From Mother's bridal gown. His brow was gone
Before she had the prescriptions filled by strangers
From another store. By then her forgeries
Were known, by nerves within her broken core
And I buried her needles along with her eyes
And burned the store to the ground. But whispers bore
Right through the grave: their bones inject my brain
With dreams of where the main line lies.

The Legacy

Sister, you left without telling me how it's done.
Your girlhood shadow, I straddled the gaps in my youth
And bowed manfully to the heroes who called
  at our house,
Watching you glide into their limbs
To a dance I could only imagine,
Then turned back to the balsa and blueprints of my
  model warplane,
Delicately gluing the parts I knew would never fit
(I had cut them so clumsily).

Past midnight in the cold bed
With the razor for cutting struts and notches glistening
  in the moon,
I would wake and hear you on the couch,
Slit by a light I had never seen,
Your coldest parts ignited by that intensity.
Deep in the groin of sleep
I saw the groans rise from their uniforms.

Now the glue is dried on my glider
And I dangle its asymmetrical weight
By a cord tied to a bulb in the ceiling;
None of your heroes will fly to my star.
Sister, I thought we were supposed to share.

The Storm
(*For Mona*)

She was sleeping in a sunken room
When I saw the twister writhing, dangling
Like a demon's tail. The core of wind
Was hurling trunks of palm trees slashed
Right past the open window, the commotion
A moan of swollen waters pummeling
The earth. The sea arose and I could see
It all, and called her to awake and come.
In the midst of all that wind she rose, and stood
Beside me at the open window, watching
The trees unfold, the sun absorb into
That funneled world. And it was like the time
I felt her breasts, and she had grown beyond
The girlhood daggers that she feared. The twister
Slashed the graves apart and she was in
My palms, my sister waking in the wind,
Remembering me, my flesh, my wild earth.

The Mound

I search for sources beyond the source—
Frozen rectangles rise and fall
That grave they told me was my sister's
Thick with grass
Blades of light
Under a sky that curved into itself
Like the cloverleaves
Of an unnumbered Interstate
The very flowers I left
Folding in toward their own roots
All signs pointing to cycles
Continuums
No ramparts for this universe
Only skies and spirals
Graves devouring grass and flowers
Sunlight tilted on the stones
Possibilities of birds
Of cradled clouds
Erupting into rain
Fusions of time and distance I must go:

No brother could compass these avenues
These endless alleys, these falling waters—
I lose my way in this rigid gridiron;
Circles and vectors must intersect your earth:
Petals and starlight—Sister—for you.

Part Six: Telling Time at Sea

Curtains of the Sea

Some people who were with me from the start,
Veiled now like the sea behind the curtains,
Moving with the ship against the grain
Of time: by degrees I saw them slip
Into a longitude inhabited
By withered waves, a high and frightened foam—
My watch disintegrates, the sextant drops
Fathoms toward their eyes, that stare at suns
The captain cannot shoot. Father dove
Deeper than the sunken stars, and Mother's moons
Dissolved.
We inch our way toward clouded latitudes.

The Voyagers

Alone we meddle with time,
Turning clocks ahead and back
While the clouds linger on the sea,
Darkening our calendars.

The earth turns and we are in darkness
(The stars remember time);
Poleward we slide toward longer light
While the waves escape to darker worlds.

Deep at the other end of light,
Out in the spaces where time escapes,
This ship is moving toward the sun
At speeds we cannot navigate—

And there in port my friend still stands,
Waiting without a watch.

The Mute, Swimming

Through petals of the jellyfish,
The clouds of the corolla,
The parachutists' strings of fire
Like curving lines of snow

Adrift on air: floating through
The ambergris, through blossoms
That shroud and hush, down halls that heave
Themselves toward stars, arcing

Along the boulevards of waves,
Touching with my eyes
The faces only once in flower,
I follow spirals, flung

Into the seas of light, with broken tongue.

The Messenger

My latest fantasy: Billy Budd
In irons, dangling above the pit in dreams
A final hour before the earth curves
Into light, and I entrusted with
His reprieve. An error in the captain's
Final charge (or some such technicality)
And I have the necessary papers for
His long swim upward into life—
He wakes (while everybody sleeps) and looks
With wonder at my key; no words, but I
Work swiftly in the lock, and he is freed
To be what time and place and silence make
A silken sailor in the dark: a heart
As tall as dockside cranes—gorged with light
And grateful, grateful, grateful.
                                                I wake in dark;
The seas are stilled.
                                I have no keys.

Part Seven: The Puritan Repents

The Donor

Driven by vectors in my loins
To project the future of my blood
I signed my cells away
In a rising battle with my flesh
Till the trajectory of love
Pierced the wall of time
And I scooped up my child in a germproof vial

Now the waves sweep past
And the flesh begins to melt from my bones
But the computers have mated my seed
Father, I have saved your line
Unswallowed by any womb
Undrowned in the woman's dark well

Yet someday I will be crossing an ocean
Seeking the wine of congeniality
And passengers will whisper behind locked hands
How my friend looks something like me
His genes carved fresh enough
For him to be my son
My son

Transparence
(*Notes from a Technician's Report*)

The brittle bones of the delicate birds
I trace now in the x-ray of my hand;
With the machine for stripping shoes and flesh from feet
I'd watch my big toe wiggle its sticks
On a plate of luminous blue deeper than sky;
Erosion in my roots has been revealed
By subtle beams of half-life molecules.
So now my radioactive glance
Peels the skin from love and leaves it stark:

The skeleton is fragile, like the birds';
The veins are blue and delicately branched,
But not quite visible, as blood dissolves.
The breasts do not appear, nor any part
I thought would blossom in the bones of love.

Postmortem

(*'Fairbanks, Alaska—Two teen-aged couples were found dead this morning in their parked car, in a local lovers' lane. Death was apparently due to asphyxiation, caused by a faulty heater, police said.'*—News Item)

The lovers on the urn were frozen there
Long before; these couples must have read it
In some English class, but they forgot,
And failed the final test. It was freezing
Beyond their heated engine; but life, not art,
Was wound into the generator. The moment
When the blood is just beneath the skin
Is warmer than the moonlight or the urn.
With windows sealed against the snow, and eyes
Pressed tight against the furnace in the thighs,
They did not see the gulls circling in
The sky, weaving through the flakes, in forms
That linked the holy hexagons. The heat
Was in eternity's designs, and they
Came through that sacred hour, safe from snow,
Carved in moonlight, cold within the urn.

In the Parlor

The spider embraced the beetle in its web—
All eight arms caressed the squirming
Carcass, the black sac stabbed with stick
Of love. The struggle of the bug, not quite
Seduced, aroused the puritan soul of me—
I ended that erotic play, with pencil
Pointed toward the lecher's tip, and down
The tumbled web came shattered bed, the partners
Of that relentless intercourse. I shuddered
To the hidden hilt of me, flicked a broom
Across the poisoned floor, said my prayers,
And dreamt of rape.

The Bachelor, at Christmas

Past the wobbling Santa in the window,
I heard the voices of trolls, elvish taunts
Of children clamped on fathers' necks. Nothing
Was visible, save those eight-foot ogres, but carved
Into the sky, a dagger dug the clouds
Apart, a stiletto of stars pierced the dark
And two cold legs of child in me bled.

To a Girl Playing Scientist
(*For Ruth*)

Jersey gypsy! You spin away our dream
On caravans to Spain, plunder Peru
And correlate Aegean kissing games.
I save my spit for poems—you laugh and take
A note on aborigines. The cream of time
I spend in hairy bachelorhood—spinster,
Margaret Mead was better at this game:
She paddled where pubescent natives rubbed,
Defined their mores till they dared not mate
Until they read her book. Come, give milk
Samoan style, erupt in buds. This art
Has taken half my heat. Take a note
On Georgians moping over poems, gypsy
Anthropologist—repeal taboos.

The Discard

My son broods
Somewhere lying formless
This night of the dying embryo
I saw his skull in the sunset hurled
Red-stained hair and finger stubs
What I had strained with every ligament to form
Till I had poured the power of my bones
In liquid pellets to the mold of love
Now ripped in muscle and chromosome
Flesh in formation, still uncurled
But a brain I sense already brooding
Rich with blood that matches mine
Searching for his father's eyes
Blind in the night of his father's love